ideals®
VALENTINE

P9-ASK-439

Hearts speak to hearts on Valentine's Day;
Love is displayed in a personal way.
Candy and flowers and big lacy hearts
Are momentoes of sweetness the occasion imparts.

Each little gift says, "I love you ... I care,"
And the spirit of romance floats in the air.
Sweet sentimental verses convey
Gifts from the heart on Saint Valentine's Day.

Author Unknown

ISBN 0-8249-1016-8 350

IDEALS—Vol. 40, No. 1 December MCMLXXXII IDEALS (ISSN 0019-137X) is published eight times a year,
February, March, April, June, August, September, November, December
by IDEALS PUBLISHING CORPORATION, 11315 Watertown Plank Road, Milwaukee, Wis. 53226
Second class postage paid at Milwaukee, Wisconsin. Copyright © MCMLXXXII by IDEALS PUBLISHING CORPORATION.
POSTMASTER: Send address changes to Ideals, Post Office Box 2100, Milwaukee, Wis. 53201
All rights reserved. Title IDEALS registered U.S. Patent Office.
Published simultaneously in Canada.

ONE YEAR SUBSCRIPTION—eight consecutive issues as published—$15.95
TWO YEAR SUBSCRIPTION—sixteen consecutive issues as published—$27.95
SINGLE ISSUE—$3.50

Publisher, James A. Kuse
Editor/Ideals, Colleen Callahan Gonring
Associate Editor, Linda Robinson
Production Manager, Mark Brunner
Photographic Editor, Gerald Koser
Copy Editor, Barbara Nevid
Art Editor, Duane Weaver

The Garden of the Heart

Let me give you one bouquet
Of hope and love and cheer
That you may know I think of you
So warmly through the year.

I wish for you a deep red rose,
That love will share your days;
A lily comes from spring's new world
For hope, in many ways.

The sunny daisy brings you cheer,
And though we're miles apart,
This message of the flowers comes
From the garden of my heart.

Virginia Covey Boswell

Valentine Magic

Three little words
That never grow old,
Magic words
Richer than gold,

Sweet valentine message
Bringing thrill ever new
To each sweetheart:
I love you!

Bernice Heisler

A Song of Love

February
Has come our way
To spend just twenty-eight short days
That melt away, yet linger on,
For February is a song
Of love wrapped up in candy hearts
And tied with ribbons, gay and smart;
It's valentines with paper lace
Addressed to ... Betsy, Sue, and Grace,
Valentines that say, in part,
"I love you; please be my sweetheart."

February
I have penned;
It is a song of love, my friend.

Loise Pinkerton Fritz

With a Little
Pinch of Love

Would you add just one thing more
To a recipe of yours
Before you give the oven door a shove?
It will make the whole thing lighter,
And your task will be the brighter
With a little, just a little, pinch of love.

In your cooking and your baking,
There is pleasure for the taking
If you first will ask a blessing from above.
Keep ingredients to the letter,
And your recipe is better
With a little, just a little, pinch of love.

Minnie Klemme

Saint Valentine's Eve

The table is littered with old magazines,
And last year's seed catalogs slyly peek
From under gay pieces of ribbon and lace;
While bright-colored papers are scattered about,

And glue pots stand yawning with wide open mouths.
Whatever is happening; why all the muss,
The clipping and cutting and making of rhymes?
Now truly! Don't tell me that you cannot guess

That tomorrow the patron of lovers appears
With a token of love from the one you hold dear;
While young hearts beat high with a will or a won't.
Here's hoping each hears from the one he loves most!

Evelyn Alcorn

Valentine's Day

Valentine's Day
Is a day for caring,
A day of love,
A day of sharing.

Sweethearts showing,
Each to the other,
How much they mean
To one another,

Kids making valentines
For moms and dads,
Parents planning treats
For lasses and lads,

Grandparents and grandkids
Doing special deeds,
Thinking up ideas
To fill special needs,

Exchanging of greetings,
Friend to friend,
Phoning or writing,
Best wishes to extend,

Remembering shut-ins
In a thoughtful way,
Cookies or candies
To sparkle up the day—

In valentine season
We each have a part
Spreading special joy
From a loving heart.

Adeline Roseberg

St. Valentine's Day

Give her a hug this morning,
Give her the old-time kiss—
From the calendar's first to final,
There's only one day like this.

Rumple her hair a little,
In the old-time tender way,
Show her you haven't forgotten...
This is St. Valentine's Day.

Never take love for granted,
Don't be afraid to speak—
While you are pouring his coffee,
Fondle his whiskered cheek.

And over his shoulder bending,
"I love you," be sure to say.
Now is the time to do it...
This is St. Valentine's Day.

If lovers at times seem foolish,
As cynics will agree,
Then this is the very morning
When foolish it's wise to be.

We all need a lot more loving,
And more of true love's display,
So, let's be a little silly...
This is St. Valentine's Day.

Edgar A. Guest

Elizabeth Barrett and Robert Browning

The courtship and marriage of nineteenth-century English poets Elizabeth Barrett and Robert Browning is one of the most romantic stories of love triumphing over seemingly insurmountable obstacles. Elizabeth Barrett spent most of her life as a secluded invalid under the domination of her wealthy, widower father. Mr. Barrett discouraged his eleven children, including Elizabeth, his oldest daughter, from marrying. Although she remained a recluse, Elizabeth began submitting her poetry to various publications, which brought her to the attention of some of the most prominent writers of her day. One of her admirers was Robert Browning, whose poetry she also enjoyed. The two authors began a long correspondence with each other, and, eventually, Browning received permission to visit Elizabeth at her home in London. Their romance flourished the following year, giving the confined invalid new strength and encouragement to venture forth gradually into the world. Browning also finally persuaded Elizabeth to become his wife, and she did so in secret, without her father's consent. One week later, she left her home forever, fleeing with her husband to Italy where they had a happy and contented life with each other. These two passionate, eloquent people left the world a wealth of moving, ardent verses in poetry and letters to each other. Mrs. Browning's "Sonnets from the Portuguese" are an especially touching tribute to her lover and a timeless expression of love for all to enjoy.

When our two souls stand up erect and strong,
Face to face, silent, drawing nigh and nigher,
Until the lengthening wings break into fire
At either curved point, what bitter wrong
Can the earth do to us, that we should not long
Be here contented?

Elizabeth Barrett Browning

I thank all who have loved me in their hearts,
With thanks and love from mine. Deep thanks to all
Who paused a little near the prison wall
To hear my music in its louder parts,
Ere they went onward, each one to the mart's
Or temple's occupation, beyond call.
But thou, who, in my voice's sink and fall
When the sob took it, thy divinest art's
Own instrument didst drop down at thy foot,
To hearken what I said between my tears—
Instruct me how to thank thee! Oh, to shoot
My soul's full meaning into future years,
That they should lend it utterance, and salute
Love that endures, from life that disappears!

Elizabeth Barrett Browning

Grow old along with me!
The best is yet to be,
The last of life for which the first was made;
Our times are in His hand
Who saith, "A whole I planned,
Youth shows but half; trust God; see all, nor be afraid!"

Robert Browning

Escape me?
Never—
Beloved!
While I am I and you are you,
So long as the world contains us both,
Me the loving and you the loth,
While the one eludes must the other pursue.
My life is a fault at last, I fear;
It seems too much like a fate, indeed!
Though I do my best I shall scarce succeed.
But what if I fail of my purpose here?
It is but to keep the nerves at strain,
To dry one's eyes and laugh at a fall,
And baffled, get up and begin again;
So the chase takes up one's life, that's all.

Robert Browning

Valentine Rendezvous

We walk into the crystal night,
Hand in hand, you and I,
Beneath the silver-chiseled stars
Caught in a frosted sky.

Ermine-cloaked pines edge the path;
I brush against boughs of white;
Sparkling snowdust crowns your head—
Oh, what a lovely sight!

Knowing that you're my valentine,
I whisper how much I care;
You tell me that you love me, too,
And we have heaven to share!

Earle J. Grant

Our World of Valentines

The beauty of a winter day
With spring just peeping through—
This is the kind of day I love
Because it brought me you.

The notes of gay operatic airs
Or stirring symphonies—
These speak to me of hours we've shared
And happy memories.

I cannot really put in words
Just what you've meant to me.
I wish you every hope and joy
That was or is to be,

Because whenever skies are gray,
Whenever they are blue,
I take my world of valentines
And find it—shared with you!

Alice Kennelly Roberts

Mother Nature's Valentine

Mother Nature sent a valentine
To everyone in town;
She dressed each pine and fir tree
In a dainty white lace gown.

Small round bushes, like quaint ladies,
Wear ruffly, white nightcaps;
The lampposts, too, look elegant
In pretty white top hats.

The landscape has a whipped-cream look
With peaks that rise and fall;
Then spendthrift Mother Nature tossed
Wee diamonds over all.

As though this still were not enough
To bring the heart delight,
She set a cardinal in the tree,
A touch of red so bright.

Mother Nature sent a valentine
To everyone I know;
She didn't need the postman;
She just wrapped it up in snow!

Kay Hoffman

Snowfall at Dusk

I found your footsteps in the drifting snow;
And swift as any hare beneath the breaking
Of cedar boughs that dangle white and low,
I sought you and I found you; and by taking

Your basket on my arm, your lips awoke
To words they would not speak before. With laughter
And hearts forgetting snowflakes on our cloaks,
We sought your door. Now in the dusk, years after,

We sit and watch the flames toss yellow embers
Upon the hearth that we have known for long;
They leap and die as swiftly as all Decembers
Since first we met. If I had trudged the wrong
Path through the whitening woods in the half light,
Would snow be more than snow, these flames as bright?

Daniel Whitehead Hicky

You and I

Many years have had their passing
Since we told each other, dear,
We would share life's joys and sorrows
Close together year by year.

We have traveled love's good highway
Over hills and through the dales
Finding sunshine on the pathway,
Smiling bravely through the gales;

Still we're walking on together,
Partners in the game of life,
Hand in hand and heart to heart, dear,
Friends and lovers, man and wife.

Life could hold no richer blessings,
As the years pass swiftly by,
Than to find us still good comrades,
Sweethearts, partners—you and I.

E. M. Brainerd

Valentine

Little painted cherubs,
Violets colored blue,
Roses pink and perfect,
Delicate in hue,
Tied with satin ribbons,
Edged with paper lace,
Crumbling, torn and brittle—
Time has left her trace.
Cherished all a lifetime,
Memory clings and stays,
Romance still remembered,
Years that seem like days!

Edith Roberts Langenau

Heart of Red with Paper Lace

Heart of red with paper lace,
Only for the hand to trace,

Angel cutouts here and there
Placed about with special care,

Neatly trimmed and folded ends,
Just for loved ones and my friends,

Chosen little rhyming words,
Gay like springtime's singing birds—

If I may, let me define,
These make up my valentine.

Anton J. Stoffle

Be My Valentine

Old-fashioned, new-fashioned sweet valentines,
Hearts, lace and flowers say, "Will you be mine?"
It's love's old story and yet ever new;
Just one more subtle way to tell to you

All that my heart holds and then reassure
That my love for you will always endure.
Really, I don't need a valentine, dear,
To prove my devotion as year follows year,

But this is a keepsake to cherish and hold
Close to your heart as you would finest gold.
Let's just be carefree and young once again,
Saying and meaning the old vows, and then

Turn to the future with love as our guide,
Taking the winding path right in our stride,
Clasping our hands in affection anew—
Valentine wishes meant only for you!

Georgia B. Adams

Silence of the Rose

Each flower has a special song to sing:
The lilies, tall and dignified and white,
Trill classic arias that thrill the night.
Some flowers have a jaunty little fling:
Petunias, zinnias, daisies shout and swing
With gay abandon, ditties rhythmic, bright,
While sweet peas, in their voices soft and light,
Croon love songs and gently arch, fluttering.

But roses do not need to sing or speak;
When they appear, the other flowers seem
To fade away; their colors dim and blur.
Here is the perfect beauty all men seek,
The mystery, the magic, and the dream.
The rose is silent; poets sing for her.

Gwendolyn Niles

Winter Peace

Looking out my window
At fields that once were green,
A sheath of white now covers
So silent and serene.

Winter has laid her blanket
Upon the earth below
With lace-doilied snowflakes
That danced as the wind did blow.

The trees, their arms stretching
Outward to the sky,
Their branches swaying in the wind,
Are whispering a gentle sigh.

The face in the moon from over the hill
Is wearing a murky grin
As if to say in looking down,
"A light for romance, I'll bring."

The snow now wears a silvery crown
That sparkles in the light;
The added enchantment of the stars
Make this a magical night.

In looking from my window
At this enchanting scene,
I'll remember winter's beauty
When earth again turns green.

Joy Dralle

Winter's Crystal Beauty

Like stardust from the heavens,
The snowflakes tumble down,
Softly embracing a sunray,
Gently kissing the frozen ground.

Gale winds scream from behind the sun
To taunt and tease the snow,
Throwing the flakes into the air
In a frozen fantasy show.

The snowflakes fall into a blanket of white,
Creating ghosts of fence posts and trees,
Melting slightly to form crystal droplets
When darkness returns to freeze.

And once night has finished its tapestry of ice
And the sun awakens to pinken the blue,
The wind sharply inhales in unsurpassed awe
At the crystallized, sparkling view.

Terri L. Bloomer

The Budding
Flower of Spring

A little girl with golden hair
And cheeks of springtime pink
Sat beside a quiet stream
Where songbirds came to drink.

In checkered coat with unmatched hat
And boots two sizes large,
She looked at me, then flashed a smile
And quickly won my heart.

The tall oak tree neath which she sat
Stood leafless in the breeze
While springtime buds were hidden still
Within the forest trees.

Above, the clouds were water-filled,
Yet I found cause to sing;
For in this small child's face I saw
The budding flower of spring.

Loise Pinkerton Fritz

The Happy Birds

No envy puts discordant note
Or sadness in a songbird's throat;
The happy birds take time to sing
No matter what the seasons bring.

They love their mates and covet not
The feathers of the other birds;
For bigger nest in higher tree
Not one would give a melody.

Mentie Du Val

Seasonal Thoughts
Valentine's Day

In February, love's as warm
As in the month of June.
It needs no breath of roses
Nor a silvery summer moon
To burnish it to throbbing glow
Or make its warmth to shine . . .
In February, love responds
To endearing valentine.

Helen Louise Williams

I made a talisman to betoken
All the words as yet unspoken,
For with laboring hands, and swift,
This one small heart is my valentine gift.

Violet Marie Larson

Red hearts on gold,
Red hearts on lace,
Two hearts caress
In sweet embrace.

Red hearts mean love;
Red hearts define
My love for you,
My valentine.

Lucile Valois

Truly, you must be
God's loveliest angel,
For His love fills your heart,
His warmth fills your eyes,
And His goodness radiates
From your soul.

Daryl Davis Henley

My heart became a valentine
Since you first met my eyes;
I send it every day to you
With quiet little sighs.

E. J. Holm

True friendship grows much dearer
As all the years unfold;
Like other things, it won't wear out
Just because it's old.

Carice Williams

A gentle smile, a gentle voice,
A kind and gentle way
Makes your life give of its sweetness
Like a lavender sachet.

Helen Virden

I've made a little posy
Of snowdrops fair and white,
And crocuses pale blue and gold
And shining with delight.

I've tied my little posy
With ribbons soft and gay;
I've put it in a pretty box,
And now it's on its way.

Tomorrow you'll receive it,
All white and gold and blue,
And if you will be true to me,
Then I'll be true to you.

Ivy O. Eastwick

My heart is a crimson locket
Aglow with a radiant pride,
For you are with me where'er I go
Forever locked inside.

E. J. Holm

There are many ways to give and receive;
To do them well is an art.
Whatever the gift, what really counts
Is the kindness and love in your heart.

It's the thought behind the gift
That makes it great or small.
To give something of self, with love,
Makes any gift best of all.

Agnes Drake

The aspens and the maples
Now have lacy frost on every bough,
And through the woods the shadows go,
Writing verses on the snow.
The tops of weeds are sealed up tight
In little envelopes of white,
And listen! In the frosty pines
Snowbirds twitter valentines.

Lavina Peterson

Quite true, it is yellowed,
Wrinkled and worn;
The writing is faded,
The laces torn;

Yet well I remember
Exquisite bliss
It gave when I claimed it
Sealed with your kiss.

Georga A. Stough

A dart, a heart, a pastel rose,
A frill of paper lace,
A cupid quite devoid of clothes
With chubby laughing face,
A white dove billing with his love,
Some sentimental lines—
Sweet potpourri of memories of
One's youthful valentines!

Margaret Davis

Valentine Memories

Lace and red ribbons,
Roses and rings,
Valentine memories are made of such things.

Handmade creations,
Great works of art,
Mother's first valentine—gift of the heart.

Small candy tokens
Lettered in red—
LOVE ME...BE MINE...YOU GO TO MY HEAD!

Valentine socials,
Box crowned with lace,
Brownies and fruit punch, hearts everyplace,

Cards animated,
Cherubs on swings
Carry love swiftly on tiny white wings.

Landscapes in ermine
Eager to show
Red-crested cardinals on branches of snow.

Cupid's been busy—
Darts sail above!
Valentine memories are fragrant with love.

Down by the rail fence
Ash tree wears snow.
North wind tells a secret—Mary loves Joe!

Dear each remembrance,
Gifts crowd the hall,
But valentine memories are dearest of all.

Alice Leedy Mason

From Valentines to Vows of Love—

American Wedding Customs

America is rich in customs, folklore, and superstitions from many countries. This is certainly evident in the origins of American wedding customs. As each national group brought to this country its own unique traditions, they became incorporated into the meaningful ceremony and joyous celebration surrounding the actual pledging of marriage vows. It is intriguing to realize that in addition to having diverse ethnic sources, many wedding symbols and activities date back to ancient times.

Here is a sampling of America's varied wedding cultural heritage.

Engagement, Betrothal, or Pledge Ring The engagement ring originated with the practice of purchasing a bride. The ring represented the prospective groom's intentions and was also considered part of the payment. Braided grass, leather, crude metals, and stones were used to fashion the earliest rings. We have medieval Italy to thank for the diamond engagement ring. The diamond was chosen as a symbol of enduring love because of its durability and beauty.

Bridal Shower A story relates that a Dutch maiden fell in love with a poor miller. Her father disapproved of the match and would not give her a dowry. The miller's friends "showered" the maiden with gifts so she could marry and start a new home without a traditional dowry.

Time of the Wedding April and November used to be the favored months for weddings, but June is now the most popular.

Some couples plan to marry when the moon is growing fuller—this is thought to bring prosperity. Others, to ensure good fortune, choose a time of day when the hands of the clock are moving upward.

Weather It is believed by some that marrying on a cloudy day means a cloudy marriage and marrying on a sunny day means a happy marriage.

Bridal Attire It is considered bad luck for the bride or a guest to wear black. The bride's white dress dates back to the Roman Empire; white was a symbol of purity. Wearing something old, something new, something borrowed, and something blue is said to bring prosperity. To the Israeli bride, blue means purity, fidelity, and love.

Bridal Veil To the Greeks and Romans, the bridal veil was a sign of youth and purity. In some other cultures, the bride wore a veil to protect herself from being seen by a jealous person or trouble-making evil spirits.

Wedding Flowers According to tradition, whoever catches the bride's bouquet will be the next to marry. In folklore, various flowers have long represented certain qualities. Bunches of herbs meant fertility and fidelity to Roman brides. Lilies have symbolized purity; roses, love; ivy, insoluble love. Victorian brides chose flowers to spell out their bridegroom's name by combining the first letters of the flower names. Robert may have been spelled out by using a Rose, an Orchid, Baby's breath, an Easter lily, a Rose of a different kind or color than the first rose, and a Tulip.

Members of the Wedding Party Having a maid of honor, a best man, bridesmaids, and ushers at a wedding is an old Roman custom. Weddings at that time had to have ten witnesses present. The entire wedding party was dressed the same as the bride and groom, so the evil spirits would become confused and would not be able to find the bride and groom.

Parents Giving the Bride Away In ancient times, the bride was considered her father's property. The parents, usually the father, arranged her marriage and actually gave her to the groom. Today the vestige of this custom means that the parents approve of the marriage.

Wedding Ring Early Egyptians used a ring to symbolize unending love. Romans preferred iron rings to symbolize the permanence of marriage. Most cultures favor gold rings for their beauty and purity.

Third Finger, Left Hand This tradition comes from England. In 1549, the English Prayer Book specified placing the rings of the bride and groom on their left hands. In medieval times, it was the custom for the bridegroom to place the ring on three of the bride's fingers in turn to symbolize the holy Trinity, and the ring then remained on the third finger or ring finger.

Bridal Garter If the bride wears a friend's garter, that friend will marry soon.

Rice Rice grows abundantly, making it symbolic of fertility and a life of plenty. It has been showered upon newlyweds throughout the years.

Wedding Bells Another superstition dating back to ancient days is the use of horns and bells to drive away evil spirits.

Wedding Cake This is another custom dating back to ancient Rome. The Roman wheat cake, which represented fertility and plenty, was broken open above the bride's head. The guests, for good luck, quickly picked up the grain that fell to the floor. During the Middle Ages, it was traditional for an English bride and groom to kiss over a cake.

Traditional trinkets may be baked in the wedding cake. Some of these items are a wishbone for luck, a heart for romance, a ring for the next person who will marry, and a coin for good fortune.

Old Shoes Centuries ago, a bride's father would give her old shoes to the groom as a sign that the groom was now responsible for her care.

Carrying the Bride over the Threshold In ancient times, it was believed evil spirits hovered at the threshold of the house, so the bride was carried over it for her protection. A superstition said that if a bride stumbled as she entered her home, she would have many ups and downs during her life.

Trousseau This custom comes from France. The bride took a bundle (trousse) of clothes and personal things with her when she moved into her new home. Later, if she had a daughter, she added to it to provide a generous dowry for her.

Honeymoon In ancient times, marriages were accomplished by capture. A man then kept his bride hidden until her relatives gave up hunting for her. Teutonic couples drank mead, a honey drink, for thirty days after their wedding or until the moon had waned.

Charivari, Chivaree, or Shivaree Postwedding serenades were popular during the Middle Ages. Crude instruments were used, resulting in rather discordant music. The French brought this custom with them to America. Often cowbells, pots and pans, guns, tin cans, and plates were used to create a noisy serenade for newlyweds at their home. Happily, this custom has almost disappeared.

Joan Turner

Something Happened to My Heart

Something happened to my heart
The day when I met you,
Something strange and wonderful.
Skies above were blue,

Steeple bells began to chime,
Birds began to sing,
Flowers popped up everywhere;
Suddenly, glad spring

Broke into its rapture, and
I knew that your love
Was as pure and perfect as
The clouds up above.

Something happened to my heart!
Now I know you're mine;
Our love shall be endless, dear,
The perfect valentine!

Georgia B. Adams

Will You Be My Valentine?

This is a very special day
To let heart's true love flow;
No matter what the weather
Love sets the heart aglow.

Love is as sweet as springtime
With sun and flowers fair;
These gifts make us remember
True love and hope to share.

Love is like spring roses
With fragrance sweet and free,
And every day is Valentine
When you are near to me.

Love is as free as birdsong,
Warm and tender with desire,
With a silent longing
Pure as a sacred fire.

There're cupids, hearts and flowers,
And love sweetly entwined,
And best of all, my darling,
You are my dearest valentine.

Mamie Ozburn Odum

Remembering

Photograph by Julie O'Neil

Gladys Taber

Few writers of the twentieth century have so touched the lives and hearts of their readers as has Gladys Taber. Though her works may not be as widely known as those of many other authors, the impact her books have had on those who love life and its deepest values is unsurpassed. It was my privilege in the spring of 1955, while on a motor tour of New England, to meet Gladys Taber and visit Stillmeadow, the home about which she wrote so lovingly for many years.

Arriving there, we were greeted by Jill who had been a close friend of Mrs. Taber's since college days and who shared with her so many years of living at Stillmeadow. We were invited into the fenced-in yard and were shown the garden, the pond, the dogs, everything that we had read about in Mrs. Taber's books.

Soon we were given a tour of the house and found it also to be as described in the Stillmeadow books. A typical example was Mrs. Taber's bedroom where her desk with the typewriter on which she had typed the books her fans had been reading for years occupied one corner. Her chair faced a window which had a view of the meadow, so she could enjoy its loveliness in all the seasons—and she loved them all.

Gladys Taber and her daughter arrived shortly. When they walked toward the house, Mrs. Taber stopped to smell a newly opened rosebud. How typical of her this act was—"to garner the perfect moments," as she had once written, and know that "those moments are happiness."

After introductions and a brief conversation, Mrs. Taber took us outside to see things of interest that we had missed. Chief among these was her champion cocker, Especially Me, whom she lovingly called Teddy. Teddy jumped up on the stone wall beside the house and refused to sit when Mrs. Taber gave the command. Her response was, "Why Teddy, have you forgotten your training?" Soon he remembered and obeyed.

Feeling that we had accepted the hospitality of Jill and Mrs. Taber long enough, we reluctantly left Stillmeadow.

After living in New York City many years and suffering the pangs of city life, Mrs. Taber and Jill and their families finally discovered the little salt-box farmhouse built in 1690 that ended their long search for just such a place. It was nestled in the Connecticut countryside near Southbury on forty acres "more or less," and after going there on weekends to escape city life, they finally made the decision to live there permanently.

Although she wrote a number of novels, four collections of short stories, four cookbooks, and several children's books, Mrs. Taber is best known for her books in which she gave an account of events that describe a simple life in and around her two homes, Stillmeadow and later Still Cove in Orleans, Massachusetts. In these two places, Mrs. Taber wrote of the people close to her and of the ordinary, everyday occurrences in her life. She put into words ideas and feelings that her readers had thought and felt but were unable to adequately express.

I was introduced to the writings of Gladys Taber in her monthly column, "Diary of Domesticity," which appeared as a regular feature in *Ladies' Home Journal* for many years. After she stopped writing for this magazine, she had a similar column in *Family Circle* called "Butternut Wisdom." In these two columns she endeared herself to readers all over the country who identified with her through her philosophy and joy in simple everyday living.

Gladys Taber's books created a world for her readers that took them out of the suffering and tragic events of everyday life. Life was not always easy for her and often contained hard work, but she considered it a great adventure and faced all challenges with rare courage.

We who have read her books know that Gladys Taber's heart lay in the simple things of life. Most important to her were her family, friends, home, books, music, the natural world around her, evenings spent around the big old fireplace, and the constant companionship of her dogs and cats who were so much a part of her life.

We who love animals have suffered with her at the loss of a beloved pet and rejoiced with her at the birth of a litter of cocker puppies. Vicariously, we have picnicked with her at her pond and walked with her through her woods. We have stood with her on a cold winter night and, looking up into a starlit sky, have felt with her the greatness of the universe and her appreciation for having been allowed to recognize its beauty in "small and finite" ways. We have stood with her under budding maple trees on a sunny April day and felt with her that no world can be entirely hopeless as long as there is an April in it.

One of Mrs. Taber's chief joys was cooking. Our appetites have been stimulated by descriptions of the meals she cooked and the recipes she shared with her readers in her columns, books, and four cookbooks.

Gladys Taber died on the eleventh of March, 1980. Until her last illness she was working on another book. After her death, her daughter edited this work and wrote a touching introduction. *Still Cove Journal*, depicting her life in and around Orleans, Massachusetts, was published a little more than a year after her death. Gladys Taber could have been describing this final book when she wrote that autumn in New England had "a sense of wistfulness because it is like a farewell party for a traveler starting on a long journey." Finishing this book the reader feels an overwhelming sadness that there can never again be the anticipation of reading another new book by Gladys Taber. But there is the realization that her many publications are always available to be read and reread, sharing again her vast store of wisdom and her ability to make everyday living an exciting adventure.

Gilbertine Moore

To My Valentine

Until you spoke, there were no signs of spring.
Your words were sudden crocuses in snow
That changed the season there before my eyes;
And as I bask now in the warmth and glow,

My heart knows in this new Elysium,
Where life is either flower or throaty bird,
I need no darts, red hearts, or paper lace.
A lighted face can best frame Cupid's word!

Angela Gall

March

Spring wears a sheath of sunshine;
Her chapeau with jonquils glows.
Crocus buds cover her feet,
For she sometimes walks in snow.

With the rustle of her skirts,
March makes her debut seem grand.
After winter's chilling blast,
She receives a welcome hand.

Mary A. Barnard

Village on Valentine's Day

Like fragile paper lace
On a valentine,
Snow is trimming our village
With an edging so fine.

Feathery flakes are falling
All along Main Street,
And there's a cheery greeting
From everyone we meet.

The scarlet-cheeked youngsters
Are coasting down hills;
Barberries are glowing
Beneath the windowsills.

Village shops are featuring
Hearts of red and pink—
Surely this is one of the nicest
Times of the year, I think!

Earle J. Grant

Valentine's Day in Our Village

Icicles fringe the village roofs;
Chimneys spout wreaths of smoke.
Frozen snow tinsels pine and hemlock
And the filigree of each oak.

Some of the shops along Main Street
Feature valentines, with fragile lace
That proclaim endearing messages
Which will bring joy to many a face.

In nearby woods the galax leaf is heart shaped,
Each a valentine from the hand of God
Nestled in its downy coverlet
That now drapes the mountain sod.

Valentine's Day in our village
Is one of the nicest times I know,
When sentimentality is showered on us
Like February's gently falling snow.

Earle J. Grant

Wintertime is the hour, lazy as blue woodsmoke
Lifting from farm chimneys,
The hour for which countryfolk long have labored,
When man and the land rest.

The
Cozy
Season

Maude Dickinson

This is the hour for braiding rugs,
For knitting mittens, piecing quilts,
For carving ax handles or mending harness,
For popping corn and eating apples,
For telling stories to the children,
Or reading beside the fire.

This is the hour for looking out on a wintry world
And savoring the coziness indoors—
At least until milking time!

Winter Woods

Fog settling softly over
Shining trees
Creates a lace fairyland
Set in crystal snow.
Long winter paths stretch
Slow and wide,
Guarded by the silent avenue
Of ice blue pines.
Snow-covered fruit tree limbs
Trace tapestry patterns
On the sky.

The dreamland shatters
In the sun,
Shining the bare black branches.
Liquid inversions
Of the world
Poise at the end
Of forest fingers.

The tender fog returns.
Its silver curtain
Draws infinities of lace
Across the woods.

Peggy Flanders

Winter Song

Deep and soft the snow lies gleaming,
Lulled by north wind's mournful singing
In the vast, imprisoned woodlands
Where a flash of scarlet winging
Adds a spark of warmth, then quickly
Vanishes in forest silence.

Fleeting, too, the sun's swift journey,
As if loath to bring new rapture
To the brook, aloof and silent,
While the fir trees strive to capture
Sights or sounds of liberation
From the season's unquelled violence.

Sing, O bitter winds of winter,
Sing your song; for, faintly ringing,
I can hear the harps of springtime,
Warmth and hope and new life bringing.

                                    Johanna Ter Wee

On Valentine's Day

Spread on the counters were valentines,
Covered with flowers and love's sweet lines;
Gilt edged and ribboned in lovely red,
Many with Cupid's adorable head.

Presents in boxes all ribbon tied,
Speaking of love that could not be denied,
Flowers and candy to brighten the day,
Fairyland opened in Valentine's way.

Into my mind comes a vision clear,
Born of a memory of yesterday-year,
When two little hands brought a heart of red,
Little soiled hands and a tousled head,

And I knew all the wealth that the store may hold,
Though priceless the jewels unnumbered in gold,
Could not purchase, in ransom, the love that shines
From those two little eyes of that Valentine.

Essie L. Mariner

The Heart You Carved for Me

You carved a heart so long ago
Upon a sturdy old oak tree,
Then turned to say, "I love you.
Will you spend your life with me?"
As I reached out to touch your hand
And our fingers did entwine,
I saw our initials in the heart—
Yours, my dear, and mine.

Though we're no longer young, dear,
I cannot say we're old, yet
I can see the silver
Shimmering in the gold.
But our love remains as strong now
As the cherished old oak tree
And the living valentine
That you carved for me.

Now as the years go passing by,
Each in its special way,
There's one place that I must go
On every Valentine's Day.
I walk the snow-swept hillside
To the sturdy old oak tree
And brush the drifting flakes away
From the heart you carved for me.

Rose Emily Houston

The Best Valentine

I remember the heart you cut on an oak
And said it was my valentine;
I remember the initials neatly carved
Just because they were yours and mine.

We felt then that not even time could erase
The message there on the old tree,
Yet you did not know what a fine valentine
You really had given to me.

It was in those moments I first realized
That I had known right from the start
That the best valentine you could ever give
Was forever carved on my heart.

Virginia Katherine Oliver

My Homemade Valentine

My little homemade valentine—
I made it for you alone.
I took the heart of a rosebud
And lovingly placed thereon

Some baby's breath from the garden
And a bunch of daises, too,
And daringly wrote upon it
With a finger dipped in dew.

I tied a ribbon of moonlight
In a love knot just for two
And sealed it twice with a kiss, dear,
And sent it straight to you.

Minnie Klemme

First Valentine

There it was, outside my door—
A heart-shaped box of red.
I quickly read the card;
"Dear Valentine," it said,
"You are my one and only love.
Will you please be mine?
If you will answer yes,
I'll be forever thine."

My young heart thrilled with joy;
Without a doubt I knew
My answer for the boy
Who spoke of love so true.
My joy was brief and fleeting—
The card was left unsigned!
How could I answer yes
If no sender I could find?

Forty years have come and gone,
And still I only guess
Who sent the candy to me
But never heard my yes!

Jewel Helms

My Valentine

I found it just the other day
With other treasures laid away—
A fragile beauty of paper lace,
The childish words, "Will you be mine?
I'll have no other valentine."
The lace that frames that childhood vow
Is torn and sadly faded now,
But Cupid smiles as sweetly as ever,
And flowers bloom in gayest splendor
On that sweet valentine of old,
Lovely in dress of lace and gold.
Dear little valentine of old,
So dear in dress of lace and gold,
I'll lay you back to dream again
Of those sweetest memories when
I, at the tender age of nine,
Received my first sweet valentine.

Mabel Lattimore Larson

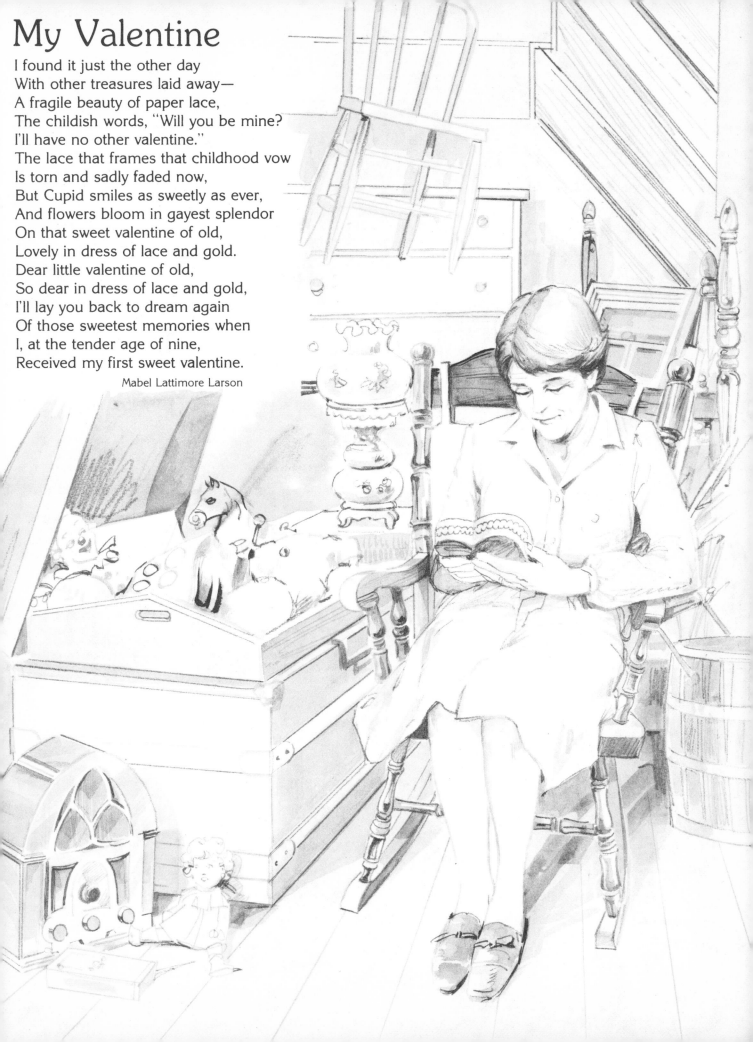

Valentine's Day Kids' Party

No one knows for sure who Saint Valentine was although Valentine's Day has been observed since the Middle Ages. There were at least three, some say eight, Valentines who had February fourteenth as their feast day, according to early records. Various legends have evolved through the ages. In an early account, one Saint Valentine was a Roman priest and another Saint Valentine, a bishop; both were martyred by the emperor for refusing to give up Christianity. According to another legend, Valentine was imprisoned and fell in love with the jailer's daughter who had become his friend. He left her a farewell note and signed it "from your Valentine." Today, Valentine's Day is an occasion when kids, moms, dads, friends, and lovers express affection through flowers, candy, and cards.

Valentine Cookie Cards and Hearts

Bake at 375° for 7 to 9 minutes.
Makes six 5 x 7-inch cookie cards and about twelve cookie hearts.

- **3 cups *sifted* all-purpose flour**
- **1 teaspoon baking powder**
- **½ teaspoon salt**
- **⅔ cup butter or margarine**
- **¾ cup sugar**
- **2 eggs**
- **1 teaspoon vanilla**
- **Red or orange sour ball candies, crushed**
- **Royal Frosting (*recipe follows*)**
- **Red and green food coloring**

1. Sift flour, baking powder and salt onto waxed paper.
2. Beat butter with sugar in large bowl with electric mixer until light and fluffy. Beat in eggs and vanilla.
3. Gradually blend in flour mixture at low speed or with wooden spoon until dough is very stiff. If needed, stir in more all-purpose flour. Wrap dough in plastic wrap; chill overnight.
4. Preheat oven to 375°. Roll out dough, one quarter at a time, between a lightly floured sheet of foil and a sheet of waxed paper, to ⅛-inch-thick rectangle, lifting paper frequently to dust with flour and turning dough over for even rolling.
5. Remove waxed paper. Cut dough with a pastry wheel or knife into a 5 x 7-inch rectangle. Cut rectangle crosswise in half if a small folding card is desired. Cut out heart shapes with floured cutters in various sizes within the rectangle or in dough around the rectangle. Remove dough trimmings from foil; reroll together at the end.
6. Place foil with cut-out dough on cookie sheet. Sprinkle cut-out heart shapes with candies.

For another design, cut a large heart, then a smaller heart in the center of that heart. Remove dough around small heart; sprinkle with candies.

7. If an imprinted or pressed design is desired, press a fork or other utensil into dough to obtain a textured or waffled effect. If you want to tie cookie cards together, make 2 small holes along one edge of each cookie with plastic drinking straw.
8. Bake in a preheated moderate oven (375°) for 7 to 9 minutes (longer for larger cookies) or until cookies are light brown and candy has melted. Remove foil with cookies to wire rack; cool completely. Gently loosen cookies from foil; store in airtight container until ready to decorate.
9. Prepare Royal Frosting. Remove some frosting into two small custard cups; tint one pink and the other green with food coloring. Spoon frosting into waxed-paper cone fitted with a plain writing or small star tip. Pipe decorative borders with white or colored frosting or write a special message on outside and inside of cards or on hearts. Or before decorating, set smaller cookie hearts on top of larger ones with frosting in between to hold in place. When frosting is dry, tie cards with ribbon; wrap in plastic wrap for giving.

Royal Frosting: Combine 2 egg whites, ¼ teaspoon cream of tartar and ¼ teaspoon vanilla in small bowl; beat with electric mixer at high speed until foamy. Gradually beat in 3½ cups *sifted* confectioners' sugar until frosting stands in firm peaks and is stiff enough to hold a sharp line when cut through with a knife. Keep frosting from drying by covering with damp paper toweling. Makes enough frosting to decorate 6 large and 12 small cookies.

It's always a gamble, but there are a number of spring-blooming bulbs that should pop out in late January or February if you planted them the preceding fall. The daffodil "February Gold," winter aconite, snowdrop, and snowflake have been my pets for many years as has been the spring-blooming crocus which ordinarily starts blooming weeks before the hybrids that are most commonly grown in home grounds.

I'm always looking for some of them to show up on Valentine's Day, and in the majority of cases they do, most faithfully.

My Favorite Valentines

Valentine's Day, the time for tender greeting,
Once led me to the mailbox, there to find
Some precious note from someone I'd been meeting
And dreaming of as beautiful and kind.

But years can change our human ways of choosing
Our dear ones to be greeted on that day;
And through the years, some of them I've been losing,
But I have other valentines that stay.

Not to the mailbox nowadays I'm going.
I will explore the garden, there to see
Suddenly above the soil in beauty growing
The valentine the good Earth sends to me.

Other loves pass, but Mother Earth forever
Returns her kindness for this love of mine;
Spring after spring, I know that I will never
Lose it—she always sends my valentine.

Dean Collins

Ocean Lore

Deep and mysterious ocean
Where fathomless caverns roar,
You draw me with your greatness;
You speak of the evermore.

You speak of the snowclad mountains
And whisper of cedar and pine.
You drink of the hills and the valleys,
The essence of woodland and vine.

What treasures from earth's great storehouse,
What substance of vision and dream
Are brought by turbulent waters
And the distant mountain stream.

What rhythm of tides and seasons,
With never beginning or end,
Is forever taking or giving
In one eternal blend!

Doris Hanks Enabnit

Snow Plant

Away in the mountains where no one might see,
A snow plant had sprouted and looked up at me.
Said I, "How'd you grow here, so crimson and bright,
Away in the forest and far out of sight?
You must be quite lonesome, so hidden out here
With no one to praise you and no one to cheer—
And specially last winter, the snow was so deep.
I think you'd just die, or were you asleep?
They tell me you sprout from some kind of a mold,
From old rotted logs and dead leaves neath the cold.
Last spring you weren't here, for I often walked by
To watch for God's beauties, wherever they'd lie.
So few come this way, and there's scarcely a sound.
You're wasted out here; you might never be found!
Why don't you rebel and grow down in the town
Where folks can admire your colorful crown?"

"Ah, no," said the plant. "'Tis the forest I like.
I point up toward God with my bright-colored spike.
'Tis true, if you'd dig, there'd be nothing to see—
No seed nor a root nor a bulb to start me.
You see, it takes winter, the snow, and the rain.
The colder they get, the more beauty I gain.
Those months when you thought I was crouched here in gloom,
I was gathering strength for my summertime bloom.
'Tis a secret that only the Lord and I know,
A mystery to man is what makes me grow.
I'm told that the city air's clouded with soot
And everything's jostled and trampled underfoot.
There're others in town to remind folks of His care—
Besides, the Creator didn't put me down there!"

Dorothy Jost

February

Garnett Ann Schultz

February, dressed in white,
Sparkled in the winter night;
Snowflakes on the chilling air
Gave the world a beauty fair,
Laughed in fun and danced in glee,
Filled with loveliness to see.

February, bright and bold,
What a lovely tale she told.
Bright-eyed youngsters, rosy cheeks,
Ice atop the frozen creeks,
Naked trees—such beauty now—
Gladness winter doth allow.

February, short and sweet,
Four brief weeks and then complete,
All that's precious, dear, and fine
Bringing us a valentine,
Can we doubt how dear you are
Neath each wondrous glowing star?

February blessings too,
Taste of spring and skies of blue,
Though so quickly snow can fly
From your ever-changing sky,
Ever precious—still more dear,
Bless you for your visit here.

Winter Interlude

Helen Virden

This moment is a pause in winter's theme;
The great composer stays the music now;
The fury of the winter's wild regime
Takes one last curtain call, makes one last bow.
So marked and quiet is the one last note,
It fades away in silence, lingering;
And in one breath the winter is remote …
We feel the great crescendo of the spring.

What will this new theme bring, what melody?
The talk of thaw in runnels and the sound
Of bright-winged birds in new-voiced ecstasy,
The grating of the plow in fallow ground?

This is the moment that we hold and treasure
Before the first downbeat of spring's new measure.

R. A. Johnson

In February

The earth is dim, the world is dark,
The midst of winter doth embark,
The days quite short and nights so long,
The frozen ground, the wind's shrill song.

In February snow mounts high,
And clouds are deep within the sky;
There's ice atop the little stream
While home fires burn and hearts shall dream.

But in the distance not too far
Our hearts behold an April star;
When flowers shall bloom and birds shall sing,
The winter melts into the spring.

In February, though 'tis cold,
We look ahead to springtime's gold;
Our minds aglow of things to be,
In February, spring we see.

Garnett Ann Schultz

It Almost Felt like Spring

It almost felt like spring today,
The world was warm and bright,
The melted snow had run away,
And winter hid from sight.

I saw a bunny on the lawn
As though he seemed to know
The wintertime was almost gone
And grass so soon would grow.

It almost felt like spring for sure,
The sky so soft and blue,
And little cloud-steps brought allure
And blessed the heavens too.

God smiled on all the world today
As sunrise touched the dawn;
A gentle beauty found its way
And slowly traveled on.

We knew so well the happiness
One shining day could bring;
With sunbeams golden in our sky,
It almost felt like spring.

Garnett Ann Schultz

Spring

Spring comes gently to the country, slipping into our lives while the last scraps of snow lie neglected, the remainder of winter's last fling. Blustery winds give way to fresh breezes that sweep away winter's gloom and usher in the gentle rains to warm the earth. Next summer's flowers stir and stretch in their winter beds, poking an inquiring green finger toward the sun to see if spring is really here . . . and finding it is so, growing and blooming, a riot of bobbing, colorful faces smiling at the world. The fruit trees don their party dresses, their full skirts fluttering in the breeze as they bow and curtsy, flirting with the staid old cedars and making brash promises about this year's harvest. All about us the bleak, colorless landscape is merging into soft pastels, the stark black trees wearing the soft fuzz of buds, roadsides becoming carpets of violets, and here and there a brazen dandelion peeping through, a sure harbinger of summer. From the new kittens in the barn and the blossoms on the apple tree comes the reminder that spring brings us a new beginning each year, that the dismal winter is over, and that the season of sweetness and light is upon us again, with the chance to sow the seeds of new friendships, new adventures, and the things that will make a summer of tomorrows warm and bright and wonderful.

Jean Marion

ACKNOWLEDGMENTS

VALENTINES (A dart, a heart, a pastel rose . . .) by Margaret Davis. Reprinted with permission of the author. I'VE MADE A LITTLE POSY . . . by Ivy O. Eastwick. Reprinted with permission of the author. ST. VALENTINE'S DAY by Edgar A. Guest. Reprinted with permission. ON VALENTINE'S DAY by Essie L. Mariner. From her book: ENCOUNTERED. Reprinted with permission of Jennings W. Mariner. THE SILENCE OF THE ROSE by Gwendolyn Niles from THE SILENCE OF THE ROSE, Copyright © 1979 by Branden Press, Inc. has been reprinted courtesy of Branden Press, Inc., 21 Station Street, Brookline Village, MA 02147. WINTER SONG by Johanna Ter Wee was previously published in THE FARMER, St. Paul, Minnesota. Our sincere thanks to the following authors whose addresses we were unable to locate: E. M. Brainerd for YOU AND I; Daniel Whitehead Hicky for SNOWFALL AT DUSK; Mabel Lattimore Larson for MY VALENTINE.

Statement of ownership, management and circulation (Required by 39 U.S.C. 3685), of IDEALS, published 8 times a year in: Feb.; Mar.; Apr.; June; Aug.; Sept.; Nov.; Dec. at Milwaukee, Wisconsin for September 1982. Publisher, Ideals Publishing Corporation; Editor, James A. Kuse; Managing Editor, Colleen Callahan Gonring; Owner, Harlequin Holdings, Inc., 306 South State Street, Dover, Delaware 19901. The known bondholders, mortgagees, and other security holders owning or holding 1 percent or more of total amount of bonds, mortgages or other securities are: None. Average no. copies each issue during preceding 12 months: Total no. copies printed (Net Press Run) 279,625. Paid circulation 53,050. Mail subscriptions 160,987. Total paid circulation 214,037. Free distribution 425. Total distribution 214,462. Actual no. copies of single issue published nearest to filing date: Total no. copies printed (Net Press Run) 181,620. Paid circulation 7,761. Other sales 155,508. Free distribution 196. Total distribution 163,465. I certify that the statements made by me are correct and complete. Donald A. Gottschalk, President.

COLOR ART AND PHOTO CREDITS
(in order of appearance)

Front and back cover, Gerald Koser; inside front cover, Colour Library International (USA) Limited; Roses and daisies, Fred Sieb; Mother's little helper, Bob Taylor; Valentine's Day tea, Fred Sieb; A hug in the snow, Alpha Photo Associates; A song of love, Fred Sieb; Snow-covered street in Sudbury, Massachusetts, Franklin Photo Agency; Floral greeting, Gerald Koser; Valentine card, Luis Machare, photo by Gerald Koser; Gift of roses, Fred Sieb; Snow-covered Wick Farm, Morristown National Historical Park, Morristown, New Jersey, H. Armstrong Roberts; Yellow crocuses in snow, H. Armstrong Roberts; Love birds, I. Bruce Edmonton; Pink rose, Colour Library International (USA) Limited; Gifts of love, Fred Sieb; Purple crocus bed, H. Armstrong Roberts; Wintry farmstead near Mayville, Wisconsin in Dane County, Ken Dequaine; Valentine nosegay, H. Armstrong Roberts; Table dressed in red, Fred Sieb; Valentine cookies, Bill McGinn; Snowdrops and aconite, Gottlieb Hampfler; Winter seascape, Portland Head Lighthouse, Maine, Fred Sieb; Fun in the snow, H. Armstrong Roberts; Grand Canyon seen from Grandview Point, Ed Cooper; Watchtower at Desert View, Grand Canyon, Ed Cooper; First flowers of spring, H. Armstrong Roberts; Crocuses, Ed Lambert; inside back cover, Fred Sieb.

Share the Joyous Season of Spring ...

Welcome the arrival of Spring in all its vivid glory with the upcoming issue of Easter Ideals. What better way to reflect upon this joyous season than with our superb offering of uplifting poetry and prose, colorful artwork, and striking photography.

Delightful poetry portraying nature's rebirth includes verses on gardening, budding flowers, blooming trees, April rain, and a host of springtime sights, scents, and sounds.

You'll also enjoy reading the story behind one of our most popular hymns in "The Amazing Story of Amazing Grace" as well as the charming piece about "Nature's Awakening" and a description of an actual little "Church by the Side of the Road."

Celebrate the splendor and beauty of Spring with an Ideals subscription for yourself or for family and friends. Share the wondrous enchantment of each successive season throughout the coming year.